THE CHESHIRE BEAGLE

THE
CHESHIRE BEAGLE

by Charles M. Schulz

An Owl Book
Henry Holt and Company/ New York

Henry Holt and Company, Inc.
Publishers since 1866
115 West 18th Street
New York, New York 10011

Henry Holt® is a registered trademark
of Henry Holt and Company, Inc.

Library of Congress Catalog Card Number: 94-73310

ISBN 0-8050-3571-0 (An Owl Book: pbk.)

Henry Holt books are available for special promotions
and premiums. For details contact: Director, Special Markets

Originally published by Holt, Rinehart and Winston in two
expanded editions under the titles *The Beagle Has Landed*
in 1978 and *Summers Fly, Winters Walk* in 1977.

New Owl Book Edition—1994

Printed in the United States of America
All first editions are printed on acid-free paper.∞

1 3 5 7 9 10 8 6 4 2

> **HOW COME I NEVER GET TO KICK?**
>
> **DO YOU THINK YOU CAN?**

> **THIS IS A PRETTY BIG BALL...**

> **I'M NOT SURE YOU'RE STRONG ENOUGH...LET'S SEE HOW HARD YOU CAN KICK...**

> **THUNK!**
>
> **AUGH!**

> **OW! OOO!! OW! OW!**

> **YOU DUMMY! YOU'RE SUPPOSED TO KICK THE BALL, NOT MY LEG!!**

> **OW! OUCH! OW!!**

> **WHAT'S GOING ON? I THOUGHT YOU WERE PLAYING FOOTBALL...**
>
> **I THINK I JUST SACKED THE QUARTERBACK!**

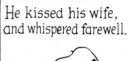

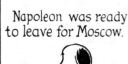

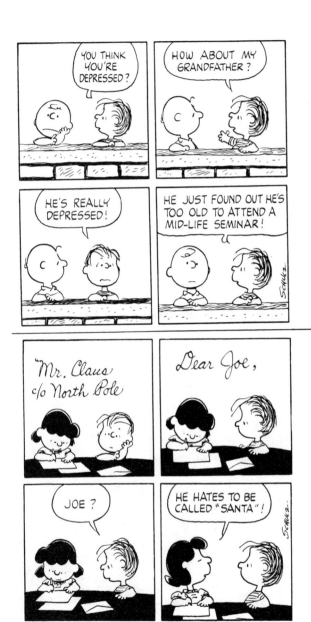

THOSE ARE BREAD CRUMBS..THERE'S NOTHING WRONG WITH EATING BREAD CRUMBS

PEOPLE HAVE BEEN THROWING BREAD CRUMBS OUT TO BIRDS FOR THOUSANDS OF YEARS

I'M SURE THEY WOULDN'T THINK THAT AT ALL

THAT WOODSTOCK IS SO PROUD...

HE DOESN'T WANT ANYONE TO GET THE IMPRESSION THAT HE'S ON WELFARE!

IT'S BECAUSE YOU STOOD STILL... IF YOU MOVE AROUND, THE SNOW WON'T STICK TO YOU

✗ WHEW ✗

SCHULZ

OH, NO...HE PROBABLY JUST MELTED... SNOWMEN CAN'T STAND TOO MUCH SUN...

WOODSTOCK IS SO SENSITIVE

HE THOUGHT THE SNOWMAN LEFT TOWN WITHOUT TELLING HIM!

GUESS WHAT, CHUCK! DISASTER TIME!

OUR TEACHER WANTS US TO READ A BOOK DURING CHRISTMAS VACATION... GOT ANY SUGGESTIONS?

ON WHAT BOOK TO READ?

NO, ON HOW TO GET OUT OF IT!

I'M NOT GOING TO HAVE TO READ A BOOK, MARCIE

SEE? "A TALE OF TWO CITIES" WAS JUST ON TV! I WATCHED THE MOVIE SO NOW I WON'T HAVE TO READ THE BOOK

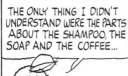

THE ONLY THING I DIDN'T UNDERSTAND WERE THE PARTS ABOUT THE SHAMPOO, THE SOAP AND THE COFFEE...

THOSE WERE THE COMMERCIALS, SIR!

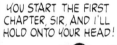

LUKE WHO?

" IN THOSE DAYS A DECREE WENT OUT FROM CAESAR AUGUSTUS..."

THE CENSUS IS SAID TO HAVE BEEN OF "ALL THE WORLD"... THIS PROBABLY REALLY MEANT ONLY THE ROMAN EMPIRE...

WHEN WE READ THAT THERE WAS NO ROOM AT THE INN, THE WORD "INN" IS BETTER TRANSLATED AS "GUESTROOM"

THE INTENTION, OF COURSE, IS TO CONTRAST A PLACE OF HUMAN LODGING WITH A PLACE FOR FEEDING ANIMALS

" PEACE AMONG MEN WITH WHOM HE IS PLEASED" IS AN INTERESTING TRANSLATION.. IT INDICATES THAT DIVINE PEACE IS NOT DEPENDENT ON HUMAN ATTITUDES...

THE NAME "BETHLEHEM" IS INTERESTING, TOO... IT MEANS "HOUSE OF BREAD"... I THINK THINGS LIKE THIS ARE FASCINATING...WHAT DO YOU THINK?

I THINK IF I DON'T GET EVERYTHING I WANT FOR CHRISTMAS THIS YEAR, I'M GONNA GROSS OUT!

SCHULZ

SNOOPY, I HAVE TO READ A BOOK THIS WEEK..

DO YOU HAVE SOMETHING GOOD?

"IT WAS A DARK AND STORMY NIGHT... SUDDENLY, A SHOT RANG OUT!"

I REALLY DON'T CARE MUCH FOR MYSTERIES...

IT'S NOT A MYSTERY, IT'S A GOTHIC!

YOU SHOULDN'T BE OUT HERE SKATING, SIR...

YOU SHOULD BE HOME READING YOUR BOOK

WHAT ARE YOU, MARCIE, MY CONSCIENCE?

IF I WERE YOUR CONSCIENCE, SIR, I'D WHIP YOU INTO SHAPE!

IF YOU WERE MY CONSCIENCE, MARCIE, I'D HAVE YOU TRANSFERRED!

ALL RIGHT, MARCIE...WHAT BOOK SHOULD I READ?

HOW ABOUT ONE BY KATHERINE ANNE PORTER, OR JOYCE CAROL OATES OR PAMELA HANSFORD JOHNSON?

FORGET IT, MARCIE... ALL THOSE AUTHORS HAVE THREE NAMES...

BY THE TIME I FINISHED READING THE AUTHOR'S NAME, I'D BE TOO TIRED TO READ THE BOOK!

YOU'RE REALLY WEIRD, SIR!

ARE YOU READING YOUR BOOK SIR?

NO, I'M WATCHING TV, MARCIE...

HOMEWORK IS HOMEWORK, SIR... WE'LL ALWAYS HAVE IT WITH US...

STOP BUGGING ME, MARCIE!

DEATH AND TAXES SIR!

LIFE IS FULL OF CHOICES!

YOU MAY CHOOSE, IF YOU SO WISH, TO THROW THAT SNOWBALL AT ME...

YOU ALSO MAY CHOOSE, IF YOU SO WISH, NOT TO THROW THAT SNOWBALL AT ME...

NOW, IF YOU CHOOSE TO THROW THAT SNOWBALL AT ME, I WILL POUND YOU RIGHT INTO THE GROUND!

IF YOU CHOOSE NOT TO THROW THAT SNOWBALL AT ME, YOUR HEAD WILL BE SPARED

LIFE IS FULL OF CHOICES, BUT YOU NEVER GET ANY!

SCHULZ

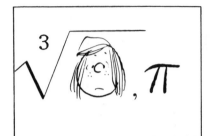

LOOK OUT FOR THE TREE!

LOOK OUT FOR THE TRUCK!! LOOK OUT FOR THE FENCE!!

AAUGH!

I HATE LOOKING AT THE WORLD THROUGH MY FINGERS!

I'VE OFTEN WONDERED IF YOU HAVE A PHILOSOPHY OF LIFE...

I MIGHT HAVE KNOWN...

"SMALL IS BEAUTIFUL!"

HALF THE FUN OF SKATING IS MEETING GIRLS...

IT'S FUN TO MEET SOME NEAT GIRL, AND MAYBE GO OVER TO HER HOUSE FOR HOT CHOCOLATE AND SIT IN FRONT OF THE FIRE...

HOW ABOUT IT, SWEETIE?

ON THE OTHER HAND, HALF THE FUN ISN'T ALWAYS HALF THE FUN!

SCHULZ

HI, SWEETIE!

HOW ABOUT YOU AND I TEAMING UP, AND DOING A LITTLE PAIRS NUMBER?

ON SECOND THOUGHT, THIS WOULDN'T BE A BAD SINGLE!

SCHULZ

YOU WANT TO SEE MY CHESHIRE BEAGLE TRICK AGAIN?

OKAY, HERE WE GO...

HOW'S THIS? YOU LIKE THAT, HUH?

OH, OH!

?

I THINK WE HAVE A LITTLE PROBLEM HERE...

I CAN'T GET BACK!

YOU'D BETTER GO FOR HELP... CALL MY OWNER! CALL HOUDINI! CALL "ALBO THE GREAT"! CALL ANYBODY!!

NO, WAIT! DON'T CALL THE...

... FIRE DEPARTMENT

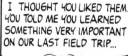

YOU KNOW, THERE'S SOMETHING FAMILIAR ABOUT THIS PLACE...

I KNOW WHY THEY BROUGHT US OUT HERE... OUR SCHOOL IS OVERCROWDED..

THEY'RE GONNA LEAVE US HERE!

I JUST FEEL LIKE I'VE BEEN HERE BEFORE...

I'LL BUY THAT! YOU WERE PROBABLY HERE IN A FORMER LIFE, AND YOU FROZE TO DEATH!

I FEEL LIKE I'VE BEEN HERE BEFORE..

WHAT'S SHE SAYING? WHAT'S OUR TEACHER SAYING?

SHE SAYS THIS IS WHAT A FARMER'S FIELD LOOKS LIKE IN THE WINTER... SHE SAYS THE SNOW INSULATES THE SOIL FROM THE COLD...

THAT'S VERY CLEVER..FARMERS MUST BE SMART..

THIS ONE SURE IS...

WE'RE STANDING OUT HERE IN HIS STUPID FIELD FREEZING TO DEATH WHILE HE'S INSIDE WATCHING TV!

I THOUGHT ABOUT YOU ALL YEAR, LINUS...

YOU NEVER WROTE TO ME OR CALLED ME, BUT I STILL THOUGHT ABOUT YOU... DO YOU THINK YOU LOVE ME?

DO YOU LOVE ME MORE THAN LIFE ITSELF?

WELL, RIGHT NOW I'M THINKING A LOT ABOUT LIFE...

SCHULZ

LINUS?

REMEMBER THE LAST TIME YOU WERE HERE? WE SAT IN THE BARN BECAUSE IT WAS RAINING, AND...

WHAT'S THAT NOISE? IT SOUNDS LIKE A HELICOPTER...

THAT'S A HELICOPTER?!

SCHULZ

ARE YOU THE HELICOPTER PILOT?!

OKAY, THIS IS WHERE YOU GO...HE'S ON A BARN ROOF... YOUR JOB IS TO GET HIM OFF, AND BRING HIM BACK!

I DON'T CARE HOW MUCH IT COSTS! BRING HIM BACK!

CHOP
CHOP
CHOP
CHOP

CHOP
CHOP
CHOP

CHOP
CHOP
CHOP
CHOP
CHOP
CHOP
CHOP

THIS IS MY REPORT ON OUR RECENT FIELD TRIP...

I HAVE A TERRIFYING STORY TO TELL! A STORY OF A DARING RESCUE!

A RESCUE FROM THE ROOF OF A BARN WHERE MY SWEETHEART WAS...

I'M NOT YOUR SWEETHEART!!

SCHULZ

THERE HE WAS ON THE SNOW-COVERED BARN ROOF!

ONE FALSE MOVE WOULD SEND HIM SLIDING DOWN TO HIS DEATH! WHAT A PREDICAMENT!

WHO WOULD RESCUE MY SWEET BABBOO?!

I'M NOT YOUR SWEET BABBOO!!!

SCHULZ

AND NOW FOR THE SURPRISE...

STANDING OUTSIDE IN THE HALL IS THE BRAVE HELICOPTER PILOT WHO PERFORMED THE RESCUE!

I'VE ASKED HIM TO COME HERE TODAY TO TELL YOU IN HIS OWN WORDS JUST WHAT HAPPENED!

NO, MA'AM...HE'S NOT MARRIED...

LET'S GIVE HIM A BIG HAND FOLKS..

OUR HERO THE FAMOUS HELICOPTER PILOT!

CLAP CLAP CLAP CLAP CLAP CLAP CLAP CLAP CLAP

I'VE ASKED OUR HERO TO SAY A FEW WORDS ABOUT THE THRILLING RESCUE...... MR. PILOT, THE FLOOR IS YOURS...

ALL RIGHT, THANK YOU MR PILOT... THAT WAS VERY INTERESTING!

OKAY, PILOT, THANKS AGAIN... THAT WAS FASCINATING, WASN'T IT, CLASS?

AND NOW, AS OUR PILOT DEPARTS, WE HAVE ONE MORE SURPRISE...

IF YOU'LL ALL GO TO THE WINDOWS, YOU'LL BE ABLE TO SEE HIM TAKE OFF IN HIS FAMOUS HELICOPTER!

CHOP
CHOP
CHOP
CHOP
CHOP
CHOP
CHOP

WHAT IN THE WORLD IS THAT?

IT'S A LIFE-SIZE POSTER OF MYSELF

I HAD IT MADE FROM A SMALL SNAPSHOT...I'M GOING TO GIVE IT TO MY MOM AND DAD AS A SURPRISE...

THAT'S A GREAT IDEA..I'D LIKE TO DO SOMETHING LIKE THAT MYSELF

DON'T! IT'S TOO RISKY...

AFTER THE PARENTS GET A POSTER, THEY MIGHT DECIDE THEY DON'T NEED THE KID!

COME AND SEE!

YOU'RE REALLY GONNA BE IMPRESSED...

WELL, WHAT DO YOU THINK?

WHO IS IT?

WHO IS IT?! IT'S GEORGE WASHINGTON! I MADE IT IN HONOR OF HIS BIRTHDAY! IT'S A MASTERPIECE!

YOU'RE JUST JEALOUS BECAUSE YOU COULDN'T DO ONE AS GOOD, AND BECAUSE YOU DIDN'T THINK OF IT FIRST!

WELL, ACTUALLY, I DID DO A LITTLE SOMETHING KIND OF SIMILAR...

I COULDN'T TELL A LIE!

SCHULZ

IF YOU PUT YOUR SUPPER DISH TO YOUR EAR, YOU CAN HEAR THE SOUNDS OF A RESTAURANT...

I CAN EVEN HEAR A WAITER TALKING...

" I'M SORRY SIR... WE DON'T ACCEPT CREDIT CARDS!"

WOODSTOCK AND HIS FRIEND ARE TALKING ABOUT ME...

I KNOW JUST WHAT THEY'RE SAYING...

THEY FORGET THAT I CAN READ BEAKS!

ARE YOU INTERESTED IN HAVING ME TELL YOU SOMETHING FOR YOUR OWN GOOD?

I'M NOT SURE

WELL, IF IT WILL HELP YOU TO MAKE UP YOUR MIND...

I'D ENJOY IT, TOO!

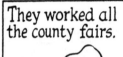

Joe Murmur and his brothers were pickpockets.

They worked all the county fairs.

How did people know their pockets were being picked?

When a Murmur ran through the crowd.

THERE'S MORE TO FOOTBALL THAN JUST KICKING THE BALL

TODAY I'M GOING TO TEACH YOU HOW TO CATCH A FORWARD PASS...

ALL RIGHT, START RUNNING!

GET WAY OUT! WAY OUT!

BONK!

OKAY, NOW HERE'S WHAT YOU DID WRONG...

I KNOW WHAT I DID WRONG! I NEVER SHOULD HAVE SPOKEN TO YOU YEARS AGO! I NEVER SHOULD HAVE LET YOU INTO MY LIFE! I SHOULD HAVE WALKED AWAY! I SHOULD HAVE TOLD YOU TO GET LOST! THAT'S WHAT I DID WRONG, YOU BLOCKHEAD!!

YOU ALSO PROBABLY SHOULD HOLD YOUR HANDS A LITTLE CLOSER TOGETHER...

SCHULZ

YOU KNOW WHAT?

I THINK I'VE LEARNED THE SECRET OF LIFE...

I WENT TO THE DOCTOR YESTERDAY BECAUSE I HAD A SORE THROAT...THE NURSE PUT ME IN A SMALL ROOM..

I COULD HEAR A KID IN ANOTHER ROOM SCREAMING HIS HEAD OFF...

WHEN THE DOCTOR CAME IN TO SEE ME, I TOLD HIM I WAS GLAD I WASN'T IN THAT OTHER ROOM ...

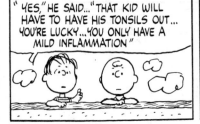

" YES," HE SAID..."THAT KID WILL HAVE TO HAVE HIS TONSILS OUT... YOU'RE LUCKY...YOU ONLY HAVE A MILD INFLAMMATION "

THE SECRET OF LIFE IS TO BE IN THE RIGHT ROOM !

HERE WE ARE...

NOW, THIS WILL BE SORT OF A REHEARSAL FOR TOMORROW NIGHT, SNOOPY...

TOMORROW IS HALLOWEEN, AND ON HALLOWEEN NIGHT THE GREAT PUMPKIN RISES OUT OF THE PUMPKIN PATCH, AND BRINGS TOYS TO ALL THE CHILDREN IN THE WORLD...

YOUR JOB IS TO BE KIND OF A PAUL REVERE...WHEN THE GREAT PUMPKIN COMES, YOU'LL GET ON YOUR HORSE, AND RIDE THROUGH THE COUNTRYSIDE SPREADING THE NEWS!

OKAY, LET'S REHEARSE IT..

HE'S COMING! HE'S COMING! THE GREAT PUMPKIN IS COMING!

RIDE, SNOOPY, RIDE! SPREAD THE NEWS!

I FEEL LIKE SUCH A FOOL!

HAVE YOU EVER BEEN "DEPROGRAMMED," SIR?

IT'S TERRIBLE! MY FAMILY HAS BEEN YELLING AT ME ALL NIGHT...

APPARENTLY IT'S ALL RIGHT TO BELIEVE IN SANTA CLAUS, BUT IT'S WRONG TO BELIEVE IN THE "GREAT GRAPE"

I THINK THAT'S "PUMPKIN," MARCIE...

I'M STILL FEELING A LITTLE DIZZY.....

MY FAMILY SAID IT'S ALL RIGHT TO BELIEVE IN SANTA CLAUS, BUT NOT THE GREAT PUMPKIN

THEY SAID YOU WERE A FALSE PROPHET

WHAT ELSE?

THAT'S ALL.. NOTHING ELSE...

WHAT ELSE?

WELL, THEY ALSO SAID YOU WERE CRAZY..

AH, WHAT A BEAUTIFUL DAY!

I THINK EVERYBODY ENJOYS TAKING A WALK THROUGH THE LEAVES ON A BRISK FALL DAY...

BONK!

WELL, ALMOST EVERYBODY

YOU NEVER LISTEN TO ANYTHING I SAY, DO YOU? I MEAN, YOU NEVER REALLY LISTEN!

OF COURSE, I DO...DON'T BE SO STUPID!

OH, YOU HEAR A FEW WORDS... SURE, YOU HEAR A FEW WORDS, BUT YOU DON'T REALLY LISTEN!

I'LL BET YOU DON'T HEAR HALF OF THE WORDS I SAY...

GO AHEAD, TELL ME WHAT I'VE BEEN SAYING...TELL ME WHAT YOU'VE HEARD...

"TO, A, OF, OH, BUT AND THE !!"

THE POLAR BEARS ARE
IN TROUBLE TODAY

DIDN'T SEE ANY
POLAR BEARS, HUH?

THAT'S A GOOD IDEA...
TRY THE OTHER
DIRECTION...

COULDN'T FIND ANY POLAR BEARS, HUH?

WELL, WHAT DO YOU THINK YOU'RE GOING TO DO?

WALRUSES?

I SEE YOU'VE GIVEN UP TRYING TO SPEAR A WALRUS...

YOU SHOULD TRY ICE FISHING

ALL YOU NEED IS SOMETHING TO CUT A HOLE IN THE ICE...

GUESS WHAT, CHUCK! MISS TENURE ACCUSED ME OF STEALING HER BOX OF GOLD STARS...

THAT'S HARD TO BELIEVE..

YOU'RE NOT KIDDING, CHUCK! IS MY STUPID ATTORNEY AROUND THERE ANY PLACE?

YES, HE'S RIGHT HERE...

"CURSE ON ALL LAWS BUT THOSE WHICH LOVE HAS MADE!"

I DIDN'T STEAL THAT BOX OF GOLD STARS, SNOOPY, BUT I'M GOING TO FIND OUT WHO DID

NOW, HERE'S MY SECRET PLAN...

I LOVE SECRET PLANS

YOU'LL WEAR THIS WIG, SEE, AND YOU'LL SIT IN MY SEAT AT SCHOOL

?

WHILE YOU'RE DOING THAT, I'LL SNEAK AROUND AND FIND OUT WHO TOOK THE GOLD STARS!

LOOK WHAT I FOUND IN YOUR WASTEBASKET, MISS TENURE... YOUR BOX OF GOLD STARS!

I'LL BET YOU THOUGHT ONE OF YOUR PUPILS STOLE IT, DIDN'T YOU?

THEY WOULDN'T DO ANYTHING LIKE THAT... ESPECIALLY THAT CUTE ONE WITH THE BEAUTIFUL HAIR AND THE FRECKLES..

AND I FOUND THE BOX OF GOLD STARS IN MISS TENURE'S WASTEBASKET

I'M GLAD EVERYTHING TURNED OUT ALL RIGHT FOR YOU, SIR...

SNOOPY DID WELL SITTING AT YOUR DESK, TOO..

HE GOT A STAR ON HIS TEST!

AAUGH!

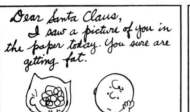

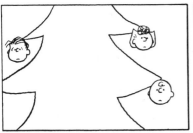

JUST BEFORE THE TEST BEGAN, OUR TEACHER GOES, "DOES EVERYONE HAVE A PENCIL?"

THIS FAT KID ACROSS THE AISLE FROM ME GOES, " I DON'T!"

THEN THIS OTHER KID WITH THE GLASSES GOES, "SURE YOU DO... YOU HAVE MINE!"

WHATEVER HAPPENED TO THE WORD "SAID"?

WHY DON'T YOU COME OVER TO MY HOUSE TONIGHT AND WATCH TV?

I'LL EVEN MAKE SOME POPCORN... WOULD YOU LIKE TO DO THAT?

NO, THANK YOU

THIS HAS BEEN A GREAT YEAR

YEARS ARE LIKE SWIMMING POOLS, CHUCK...

WE JUMP IN ONE END, AND WE SPLASH AROUND UNTIL WE REACH THE OTHER END

HOW WAS YOUR YEAR, CHUCK?

SOMEBODY LET ALL THE WATER OUT!

WELL, I GUESS I'M ALL SET FOR WOODSTOCK'S NEW YEAR'S PARTY...

I HAVE MY TOP HAT...

MY FANCY TIE...

AND MY PARTY SMILE!

HOW MANY SKATING TESTS ARE THERE, SIR?

EIGHT, MARCIE, AND THEY GET HARDER AND HARDER

SOMETIMES I THINK THE ONLY THING THAT KEEPS ME GOING IS THE ENCOURAGING WORDS OF MY COACH...

GROWL, *SNARL,* SNAP, *GROWF,* BARK, *WOOF!*

OKAY, BEAUTIFUL, GET OFF THE ICE!! WE'RE GONNA PLAY HOCKEY!

HOCKEY?! GET LOST, NECKHEAD! I WAS HERE FIRST!!

YOU WOULDN'T LIKE TO GET HIT WITH A HOCKEY STICK WOULD YOU, BEAUTIFUL?

HOW WOULD YOU LIKE TO BE FORCE-FED A PAIR OF GOALIE PADS?!

LISTEN, BEAUTIFUL, GET YOUR STUPID FIGURE SKATES OFF THE ICE! WE WANNA PLAY HOCKEY, SEE?

WE HAVE TEN HOCKEY STICKS HERE TELLING YOU TO "GET OFF THE ICE!"

OH, YEAH? COME ON AND TRY SOMETHING! ME AND MY COACH'LL TAKE YOU ALL ON!!

I THINK I'LL GO HOME.. I HAVE SOME CHAIN LETTERS TO WRITE...

THOSE HOCKEY PLAYERS ARE TRYING TO CHASE PEPPERMINT PATTY OFF THE SKATING RINK!

DON'T LET 'EM GET AWAY WITH IT, SIR!

I'LL HELP YOU

AAUGH!!

I DON'T EVEN REMEMBER WHAT HAPPENED, SIR...

WELL, THOSE HOCKEY PLAYERS WERE ABOUT TO GIVE ME A ROUGH TIME, AND YOU CAME RUNNING OUT TO HELP ME, MARCIE

BUT I SLIPPED AND FELL ON THE ICE, HUH?

I'LL SAY YOU DID!

LET'S GO BACK AND SHORTEN A FEW LIFE SPANS, SIR!

LATER, MARCIE, LATER

GUESS WHAT, SIR..WHEN I GOT HOME AND TOLD MY MOTHER ABOUT FALLING ON THE ICE, SHE CALLED THE DOCTOR...

HE TOLD YOU TO TAKE IT EASY, HUH? WELL, THAT MAKES SENSE..CAN I GET YOU ANYTHING?

NO, THANK YOU, SIR... I'M JUST GOING TO LIE HERE, AND TRY TO READ "PILGRIM'S PROGRESS"

IF THE FALL ON THE ICE DIDN'T GIVE YOU A CONCUSSION, MARCIE, THAT WILL!

NOW IF SOME KID COMES UP, AND STARTS ASKING ABOUT A RULER, YOU HOLD HIM OFF...

HOLD HIM OFF?

YES, YOU HOLD HIM OFF WHILE I RUN FOR IT!

WHAT IF HE TRIES TO HIT ME?

REASON WITH HIM

TELL HIM HIS STUPID RULER WOULDN'T HAVE BEEN ANY GOOD AFTER WE SWITCHED TO METRICS, ANYWAY!

IT WAS A TWELVE INCH RULER? I SEE...

IT'S THAT KID FROM SCHOOL AGAIN... HE WANTS HIS RULER...

SHALL I TELL HIM A TRUCK RAN OVER IT?

ASK HIM IF HE'LL SETTLE FOR THREE FOUR-INCH ONES

WELL, I HOPE YOU'RE SATISFIED, BIG BROTHER.. I BOUGHT THAT STUPID KID A NEW RULER...

GOOD FOR YOU... AND I HOPE YOU LEARNED A LESSON ABOUT RETURNING WHAT YOU'VE BORROWED

I SURE DID

IT'S A LOT BETTER THAN GETTING PUNCHED OUT!

HEY, STUPID CAT! YOU WERE OUT KIND OF LATE LAST NIGHT, WEREN'T YOU? WHAT WERE YOU DOING, STAR GAZING?

NO, YOU'RE SO STUPID YOU PROBABLY DON'T EVEN KNOW WHAT A STAR LOOKS LIKE!

HEE HEE HEE

SLASH

WELL, I SUPPOSE THE FIRST THING WE SHOULD DO IS HAVE A LOOK AT YOUR HOME-OWNER'S POLICY...

WHAT KIND OF A TASSEL CAP DO YOU CALL THAT?

IT DOESN'T EVEN HAVE A TASSEL!

HOW CAN YOU HAVE A TASSEL CAP THAT DOESN'T HAVE A TASSEL?